Sammy's Special Delivery

Letters from over The Rainbow Bridge

Penny J. Maxson

Printed in the USA

Copyright 2017 by Penny J. Maxson
All rights reserved

ISBN-13: 978-1977932730
ISBN-10: 1977932738

I would like to thank
a special author friend,
Eugenie D. West,
for helping me brainstorm
for the title of this special book.

I think the title
fits the message perfectly.

WHO IS SAMMY?

Sammy was, and is, the most wonderful companion and "head of household" anyone could ever have. At least that is my opinion. Sammy loved our family and looked over us vigilantly for the better part of sixteen years. His passing over the Rainbow Bridge has left a never replaceable void in our hearts and our home.

Young Sammy
when he first came
to live with us.

Sammy's Special Delivery

A collection of precious

"Letters from over the Rainbow Bridge"

Hi Mommy!

Wow! Wow! - Thank you for letting me out of that old sick body! Wow, Mommy! It is so nice here. I am so happy to be up here.

I can jump and do somersaults again. Whee!!! I have lots of butterflies to chase! I don't have to wait for anyone to play with my string. I just jump and play with all the neat butterflies. They aren't on a string, so it is a real challenge to catch them. When I catch one, it just gives me a kiss on my nose and flies away.

You will never guess who came running to greet me. Yep. The Kid came running and jumped right on my back.

I didn't see him at first. But I knew that familiar thump on my back.

Oh Mom, I was soooo happy to see Jasper again. We rolled all over the grassy yard together.

And guess what? – Jasper has TWO good eyes now. He feels all perfect too. His tummy doesn't hurt anymore. We had so much fun playing together.

I asked if he knew where Brittany was. He took me to where they always chase each other around the beautiful trees.

Oh, Mom, she is so beautiful!! She ran to us and just licked us all over. We ran and ran and then Brittany laid down in the grass and Jasper and I laid down with her to rest. It was so peaceful. We are so happy to be back together again.

It was a good first day here. I love you Mommy. Please tell Daddy I love him too. I am so sorry to see you both crying so much. Please don't keep crying. You are the best Mommy and Daddy a fur kid could ever have.

Thank you for taking such good care of me when I was getting so sick. You never fussed at me when I made any mistakes. I always felt bad that I caused so much work for you. But you always treated me with so much love.

I am all healed now and so very happy to be with Brittany and Jasper again.

Please always remember our fun times and please don't keep crying.

Thank you so much for sending me here with Brittany and Jasper.

I will keep writing more letters to you. I have not left you. We will all be waiting for you and Daddy to come and live with us one day.

Love you, Sammy

Brittany was Sammy's first love in our house

Sammy and Jasper were soulmates from the very beginning

Hi Mommy!

I was watching you and Daddy this morning when you were lying in the bed talking about how much you miss me. I am sorry I can't tuck you in bed like I used to. Just remember that I am really still with you both. Just close your eyes and you can still hear me purring very near you. I still love you and I will never really leave you. I am in your hearts forever.

I always had so much fun waking you both up in the mornings. You and Daddy were always happy to see me and I loved all the petting and all those wonderful back rubs you both gave me.

That was a really nice picture you put on Facebook of Brittany and Jasper and me. I hadn't seen that picture for a long time. I am so glad you have so many great pictures to remember us by.

Oh yes, remember that poor little skunk that was run over the other day? He told me to tell you he could see how badly you felt for him. However, he wants me to tell you that he is just fine now. He made a very quick trip up here, no suffering at all. He is really cute and very nice. He doesn't even have a bad smell up here.

Everything is so beautiful and it smells so good. The trees are all so beautiful and the grass is so green.

There are no dangers here at all. No real doors for us to run in or out of. We are just free to go and play everywhere.

I really love it here Mommy. I can feel how sad you and Daddy are. I wish you could stop hurting so much. I see you both are still watching for me at the door when you come and go. I guess that is natural. It had been almost sixteen years of doing that every day. It will get better for you both. I promise.

Jasper told me to tell you he is really sorry for the time he ran out the front door when Daddy was setting the trash outside. He really didn't mean to scare everyone so much. He had no idea where that door went to. When he found himself outside in the cold, he really got scared and that is why he just hid under the bush. He was so happy when Daddy found him. He said to tell Aunt Judy thank you for leaving school that day to come and help get him safely back in the warm house. He was a little stinker. Always so much fun. He still is. He is always running everywhere. It is so good to see him so healthy and so happy.

Well Mom, I guess I will get back to chasing those beautiful butterflies. They are a lot of fun.

I love you and Daddy so much. And remember, I am always with you. You just don't have to worry about tripping over me now.

And please stop crying. I am really ok.

Love you, Sammy

This is the picture
Sammy was talking about
that I had placed on Facebook.
My three beautiful babies
are reunited over the
Rainbow Bridge

Hi Mommy!

I see your suitcase is out. I don't have to be so afraid of you leaving me anymore. Now I can see everywhere you go.

I hear you and Aunt Judy are going to a cat show this weekend. I am sure you will have fun. I know it will be hard on both of you. Just remember, I am so very happy up here. I am always with you and I will be watching over you all weekend.

I have noticed you and Daddy are still looking around for me at times. It will just take time to retrain yourselves so you stop worrying about tripping over me.

Oh Mommy, I almost forgot to tell you I met the nicest, cutest puppy up here. He told me he had been expecting me and wanted to meet me. He said he was one of my puppy brothers.

His name is Champ! He told me all about how you got him and what a wonderful life he had with you and Daddy. He told me all about Smokey and Skippy too! Wow! You and Daddy have had a lot of fur babies. But

I am so happy I was your very first cat fur baby. That makes me feel really special.

Please be really careful when you go to New Jersey for the cat show.

Tell Daddy I love him too!

Lots of love, Sammy

This is our precious,
rambunctious, Champ
Such a special little guy

Hi Mommy!

I have to say it has been so much fun watching you and Aunt Judy on your trip to New Jersey.

I never knew what you two were up to when you would pack your suitcase and leave me for those days. Now I understand. Whenever you come to live here with us, you will be able to understand lots of stuff you could never figure out down there.

I've been watching Daddy work really hard on his yard sale. He has still been watching the door for me. He is such a good Daddy. I felt sorry last night when he went to bed and I was not there to tuck him in when he was all alone. He did pretty well sleeping alone.

Oh Mom! I love being here. It is so much fun! Remember the somersaults I used to do? I can really do good ones now. I also have real butterflies and even birds to chase after. They love playing with me. There is no furniture for me to crash into either. So much green grass and soft clouds to catch me.

Brittany said to tell you "Hi". She remembers my somersaults. She always wished she had all that energy I had back then. But now she is able to almost keep up with me. She is so funny to watch. Mom, she runs like a girl. I guess maybe it is because she is a girl. I sure do love her.

Jasper has been running after birds all day. Now that he has two good eyes, he doesn't trip over everything. The birds love to play with him. They chirp and sing for him. He is such a pretty boy.

He still loves to run up behind me and jump on my back. I guess that will never change. I don't get upset with him like I did down there. I just turn around and chase him all around the beautiful, soft grass. Nobody gets upset up here. Everyone is happy all the time and we all love each other very much.

Tell Daddy I love him. And be sure to tell Aunt Judy I hope she has a good day at her cat show. I will be watching you both. That is when I am not playing with my favorite butterflies.

I love you, Sammy

This is one of Sammy's
pictures from his book
<u>Sammy Goes on Tour</u>
Written by his Aunt,
Judy S. Walter

Hi Mommy!

Just checking in with you. I have been watching Aunt Judy selling all those books today.

Wow! She sure does tell my story really well. I am happy you both are having a good day. Brittany wants to know why there is no book written about her. I told her she is mentioned in at least one of my books. Maybe one day she will have a book written about her. She is just so pretty and so loving. I was so happy when she wanted to have me as her very own kitty when I was so young and looking for a forever home. She always smells so good and she is so soft.

She was telling me about how you crawled under that dirty porch and pulled her out of that mud. She felt so bad and was so scared. She said she felt so much better when you took her home and gave her a bath. She knew she wanted to stay with you forever. I am so happy for her that you and Daddy found her

Well Mom, I will go for now. I love you so much and I hope my letters make you feel better every day.

Everyone up here sends their love.

I love you, Sammy

Hi Mommy!

I've been watching you and Aunt Judy today at the cat show. I saw you talking to that nice man about his book, The Kitty. I will have to look Kitty up. I am sure he is around here close. He looks like a really handsome guy.

Jasper and I have been chasing birds all day. It is a lot of fun. There are so many birds and so many colors. They all make different noises and they are really funny too. There should be bird shows too. There are so many pretty ones up here. And Mom, some of them actually talk too. They say neat and funny things like . . . "Hey there"!, "Polly want a cracker"? . . . "Hello". Some of them were taught to say some bad words too. They can't do that up here though. But they don't care. They know lots of other good words.

Please tell Daddy not to work so hard. I watched him doing his yard sale yesterday. He was really tired. When he went to bed last night he really went fast asleep. It was good for him that I was up here. He didn't have to get up so many times to look after me. Now he knows I am well and safe up here.

And Mom, we have beautiful rainbows up here all the time. We don't have to get wet at all to see them. It is really great here. So many pretty things and so many nice people. Everyone up here loves dogs and cats and all the other animals too. And no one up here is allergic to any of us. That is so wonderful.

I can still see how much you miss me. Just remember, I am all well now. I love you Mommy. I was such a lucky boy to have you and Daddy as my parents.

Thank you for holding me so tight and always petting me those last few months. I am so glad you could understand how hard it was getting for me. Your love and patience were so good for me. I hated to leave you, but you knew it was my time to be healed and to go over the Rainbow Bridge. I felt so secure in your arms. I knew I was safe and loved. Thank you so much for your love.

I will be watching you and Aunt Judy on your way home. Please be safe. Tell Aunt Judy I love her too.

I know you will be happy to be back home with Daddy tonight. Please give him kisses on his nose for me.

I love you, Sammy

Hi Mommy!

I know you were looking for a letter from me yesterday.

I was so busy celebrating my first full week up here with my special friends and family.

I did take time to watch what you and Daddy were up to a few times during the day.

I know you both really miss having me to tuck you into bed every night. I am sure it will take a while to get used to going to bed without my purring in your ears. I really loved doing that for you. We don't really have beds up here. We just curl up anywhere we want and fall asleep. It is so warm and comfortable up here. The grass makes a really wonderful place to sleep. We can stretch and roll all around and there is no bed to fall off.

Thank you for always putting the extra pillows on your bed so I wouldn't fall off. That one time a long time ago when I fell off backwards and hurt my back was not fun at all. I always knew how bad you felt about that. I did enjoy all the hugs and kisses you gave me, and all the rubbing you did for my back. That felt extra good to me.

I was so happy when you and Daddy put those extra pillows and stuffed animals along the edges of your bed. That was always a lot of work to put them up every morning and take them down every night. I knew you always did it because you loved Jasper and me so very much. We were such lucky boys to have you and Daddy as our parents. You are still our parents because we still live in your hearts.

Well, I am going to go looking for the cat in the book you read. There are so many wonderful cats up here. It might take a while to find him. I will let you know when I see him. Kitty is his name. I am sure I will find him. He seems like a really great guy.

I love you Mommy. I know you still keep looking for me at the door. I can see you hesitate and then remember that I am not there now. Thank you for being such a dedicated Mommy. You took such good care of me. Talk later Mom.

I love you, Sammy

This was Sammy and Jasper's
secure and safe bed

Hi Mommy!

I could tell how sad you were all day yesterday. I am so sorry you miss me so much. I know you are trying very hard to just keep going forward and find a happy place again.

I know how hard it was for me when Brittany left us. I worried about her for a very long time. And I missed her so much. I always tried to remember all the things she taught me. I always tried to take good care of you and Daddy and Jasper just like she showed me. I wanted to make her proud of me. She told me the other day that I had done a perfect job.

I really felt awful when we lost Jasper Mom. I just could never be really happy again after Jasper left us. We were a happy family of four. Nothing was ever as good after he left us.

I know how hard you and Daddy tried to make me feel better. You both worked so hard to make me happy. I thank you so much for all you did for me. I know how sad you both were too.

I made it almost three years after we lost Jasper. I know we were both getting to be older boys. We just can't live down there forever, even though we all hate to leave our wonderful families. There just comes the time for us to come up here.

I knew my time to leave you was coming very soon. I just felt so bad and could barely eat or even walk through the house. I really did not want to leave you and Daddy.

You and Daddy were so wonderful to me. I really loved our times lying on the bed. All that petting and rubbing me all over felt so good. You always knew what I wanted when I was asking you to lie down with me. I could hardly wait for you to get home when you went away during the day. I always knew you would come home and lie down with me. Sometimes it was only for a few minutes but it was always a warm, happy time for me. It was a neat game that I really did enjoy.

Everything makes sense to me now. I know why Brittany had to leave. She has told me about her terrible headaches and how confused she was getting. She was so happy to come up here that day. She didn't want to leave us, but she was all healed and felt all brand new when she arrived here.

Jasper told me the same thing. His eye was causing him so much pain. He always had tummy issues and it was all getting worse every day. He just was feeling so miserable trying to keep going down there.

We are all so sorry you and Daddy are so sad. We can see how lonely you are. It will get better as time goes on. We know you will never, ever forget us, but please try to feel better and remember all our fun times together.

You did the most perfect thing for each one of us. We love you for being such a good Mommy and Daddy. We miss you too, but it is so much fun up here, we can't be sad.

Please give Daddy a big hug and some puppy and kitty kisses from us. Try not to be so lonely and sad.

We all love you, Sammy

Sammy in his Daddy's arms the day before he travelled over the Rainbow Bridge

Hi Mommy!

Wow! You and Daddy have sure been extra busy the last couple of days. I am glad to see you busy and not worrying so much about me.

I do see every time you look for me, when you come and go in and out of the doors. I saw you look in your bedroom, and then realize you don't have to do that anymore. I am safe and happy up here.

I was watching you this morning when you used that great smelling powder. I always knew when you used it. It smelled so good. I could smell it from wherever I was. I always came running to get a whiff and try to lick any spilled powder up off the floor. Now you can use it and not worry about me licking it up for you if you spill any.

I haven't run into the cat named Kitty yet. I am sure we will meet up soon.

I saw that great card Dr. Jeanine and her office sent to you and Daddy. I liked it when she said I was a "super star cat". I sure did love her. I always purred as loud as I could for her. She always liked my purring. I always was a gentleman for her because I knew she loved me, and you only took me to see her when it was important.

Jasper caught two butterflies at the same time today. They both kissed him on his nose and flew away. He was so proud of himself. It is so much fun watching him play.

Well, I am going to go see if I can find Kitty anywhere. It would be fun to meet him.

I love you Mommy. Please tell Daddy how much I love him too.

Love, Sammy

Hi Mommy!

I have been watching you and Daddy. You both have been really busy, as usual.

I am sorry you have been missing me so much. I really am happy up here. It is just a perfect place for me. Please don't worry about me. I know it is hard for you. Just remember all the great fun times we had.

Do you remember the night the tree fell in our back yard? I tried so hard to wake you up. I MEOWED as loud as I could and I kept smacking you on your arm. When that didn't work, I started knocking things off your night stand. Finally, that worked. I found out that was a much better way to get your attention.

I will never forget how shocked you were when I showed you out the window! It sure took a lot of work to get you there. I kept telling you it was really important!

You were so proud of me. That made me feel so good. I always loved it when you bragged to everyone about how smart I was.

Yep, we have so many great memories to

smile about. I had so much fun being your fur baby.

Well, I have to go. Jasper has been chasing Brittany all over the place today. When she lies down to let him catch her, he curls up beside her and they take a nap together. I love lying beside them and purring them to sleep, just like the good times at home with you and Daddy.

I am happy here Mom. Give Daddy a kiss on his nose for me.

I love you, Sammy

Hi Mommy!

I did it! I found him! I found Kitty! Mom, he is so nice! We have become great friends today. We shared our life stories and really are a lot alike. He misses his Daddy a lot. But he said he is happy his Daddy let him come up here when he did. He had been really sick for a while too. Kitty has been here a little over two years now.

Mom, you know I never really cared for orange kitties. I would always growl when I saw one in our back yard. Well, now I have an orange kitty as a best friend!

Like I said before, you can really understand stuff when you get up here. Now I am not upset when I see orange kitties. I have no idea why I didn't care for them. Must have been something in my earlier life that made me feel that way. But that is over now. Orange is good!

Champ was telling me today about his other fur brother named Smokey Bear. He said they were great brothers down there when they were with you and Daddy.

We are going to look him up and see if he has met Brittany yet. He seems like he would be a great fur brother. I will let you know when I see him

I love you Mommy. Be sure and tell Daddy, I love him too.

Love you, Sammy

Hi Mommy!

I see Kim is in Florida for a vacation. I always loved it when Kim petted me. I was a little shy with her for a while, but when she visited more and more, I got used to seeing her. It was always nice when she would come to see me when I was stuck in the bedroom because we had company. I know you were protecting me from getting out the door and getting lost. But I always wanted to visit with everyone.

I am so glad Kim came and spent time with me just before I left you all. It was a real special time with all of us sitting in your office. You all sat and talked with me. I was very happy when Kim sat on the floor with me. It even made me purr.

Please tell Kim I love her too. I hope she has a good vacation. I bet Florida has a lot of butterflies and birds. But not as many as we have up here.

Love, Sammy

Hi Mommy!

Just wanted to tell you how much I love you! I have been looking around for Smokey Bear. Everywhere I look they tell me he was just there a little while ago. He seems very popular up here. They say he looks a little bit like a German Shepherd. But they also say he has one brown eye and one blue eye. So we think he is part Husky too. I bet he is very handsome. You always called me your little German Shepherd. Hmmm . . . does that mean we look alike? I guess we will find out when I see him.

Jasper was chasing a bird today and he climbed right up the tree after the bird. When the bird flew away, Jasper leaped out of the tree after the bird. Thank goodness there are plenty of fluffy clouds all around here. He was falling really fast when he landed on a great big cloud. He looked so funny all sprawled out in that cloud. Like I said before, we are all safe from any dangers up here. Everyone was laughing and so happy Jasper landed softly in that cloud.

It has been a good day today. I did see that you read a couple of my letters to Aunt Judy today. She seemed to really like hearing from me too. Please be sure and tell her that I love her.

I remember the times when I was just a little guy and still hanging around your house. She would open the bathroom window and let me in so she could pet me. I just knew one day I would be living inside with Brittany and you and Daddy. Aunt Judy always loved me too. I knew I had found my forever home with you all.

I could tell everyone in the house loved me. I did have to work a little harder to convince Daddy. But he really came around when I climbed to the top of that screen and started screaming because I couldn't get down. I remember him telling you to come and get me down and bring me inside.

I loved being inside with you and Daddy and Brittany. Aunt Judy was so happy to have me inside, especially since she had been smuggling me in the bathroom window.

I always felt so loved. Thank you for always loving me so much. I always felt so happy when you told me I was the best kitty in the whole world. I did always try to be a very good boy. Of course, you always told Jasper he was the best kitty in the whole world too.

I have to say we both were really good boys. We never hissed or spat at anyone. We never smacked at anyone or growled at them. Jasper always ran, but he got better over the years. It was so easy to be good for you and Daddy because you were so good and loving to us. We never felt afraid or insecure at all.

Well, now that Jasper has caught his breath from all that running and climbing and trying to fly, we are going to meet up with Brittany and take a nap together. We may also invite Champ for a nap too. He is one very bouncy boy full of energy. He is always having fun chasing anything that moves. It is so funny when he barks, his whole body lifts off the grass. We love to spend time with him. He has really cute ears too! One stands up and one lays down. It gives him real personality for sure.

This has been a long letter. I had lots to tell you today.

I will write again soon. I love you Mommy. Give Daddy kisses from all of us.

Love you, Sammy

Hi Mommy!

I can see how discouraged you are today. I saw you talking with the lady at the pet store. You were trying to be so brave when you told her about me. You were wishing you had me back. Mommy, I really haven't left you. Maybe I am gone physically, but I love you. You always did your very best for me. Please don't worry so much and wish you could have done something better. You always did the best for me. You are missing me a lot today. I wish you could just remember how happy I am up here. I am still with you in your heart. You just don't have me to trip over.

Just close your eyes tight tonight and I bet you can hear me purring in your ear. I want you to feel better. I am happy and having so much fun up here. Please remember that.

Jasper and I have been looking all around for Smokey Bear. I think we are getting close to finding him. It is a really big place up here. When we find him, we will let you know.

Daddy has been working hard. He always works really hard. I do miss our little naps together on the bed. At least I made you both take little naps with me and that helped you two to get a little rest during the day.

I have so much energy now I don't need to nap much during the day. Jasper and I do love to lie down sometimes with Brittany. She is so soft and warm to lie with. We really love her.

Did I tell you, I have all my hair back on my arms and my side. I look pretty handsome, just like when I was a kid.

You always loved me and kissed me all over no matter how much hair I lost. You made me feel so handsome and so loved. Thank you for loving me so very much.

I remember how much you were kissing me in Dr. Jeanine's office that day I left for the Rainbow Bridge. I saw you still kissing my cheek and my nose even after I was gone. A boy just could never feel as loved as me. You were always loving and hugging and kissing me, even when I was trying to get away sometimes. But I always really loved your hugs and kisses. They made me feel so special and I always knew how important I was to you and to Daddy too.

I wish you could see the pretty rainbows we have up here. They are all so nice and so are the pretty flowers and trees. The grass is so green and soft. And the grass never needs to be cut and it never gets all crunchy like ours did down there. Daddy would never have to cut it or water it and it would stay all pretty. Daddy always worked so hard to keep the yard looking nice. He could take it easy if he had this kind of grass. Never have to mow or trim it. But I think this kind of grass is a special kind for up here. It sure does make a boy feel safe and secure. Nothing to hurt us at all. And we are never lonely or sad. We all love it up here.

Well, I am going to go looking for two special birds I ran into the other day. They came to play with Jasper and me. Their names are Happy and Punchy. They told us they were your feather babies a very long time ago. They said you were just a kid when they lived with you. They said to tell you they loved being your birdies. Happy is a pretty blue parakeet and Punchy is a green and blue parakeet.

They said they were sure you would remember them. They were telling me that you taught them to talk too. They say all good words.

Happy told me to tell you that his foot is all healed now too. He remembers the day he landed on the hot toaster. He said it really did hurt. He felt better after a while, but he still had a little limp when he tried to walk. Happy told me all about your own Mommy and Daddy. Wow! That really was a very long time ago.

I love you Mommy! I always will love you. Please give Daddy kisses on his nose. And try to close your eyes and listen for my special purring tonight. Please try not to be so sad.

I love you, Sammy

Hi Mommy!

You sure have been really busy the past couple of days. It takes a lot to keep up with you. Now I can always see where you are. I know why you left me alone so many times down there. I always missed you and Daddy when you all went out the front door and took so long to get back home. Now I know you and Daddy were always working really hard.

I am never lonesome up here. It is so nice and everyone takes care of each other. We can see what all our friends are doing. We never sleep alone, or have to stay alone ever. It is so comforting up here.

I hear you are going back to an airport tomorrow. Please be careful when you are driving. It was raining so hard down there today. It was kind of hard to see through all the rain. But I kept watching you. I love you Mommy. I love being able to see everything you and Daddy are doing now.

I especially like it when you both are happy. I do not like to see you both so lonely and missing me so much.

Just always remember how happy I am up here. And I am still with you. I live in your heart in a very special place.

Happy and Punchy have been looking all over for Smokey Bear. They said they would let me know when they find him.

Well, I am going to go now. I want to help Jasper catch a few butterflies. Maybe I can keep him on the ground and not climbing trees. The butterflies don't fly quite as high as the birds do.

I love you, Sammy

Punchy & Happy

Hi Mommy!

Wow! That was a very nice compliment from Aunt Judy's friend Sue.. I always loved it when she came to visit.

Her purse always smelled so good. I loved to curl up next to it and rub my face all over it. She always smelled so good. And she really liked me a lot.

I liked it when she told Aunt Judy that I was an "exceptional cat". I am glad she felt that way about me. Please tell her I said, "Thank you."

Well, we finally located Smokey Bear. He still goes by the name Smokey. He is really a great boy. I love it that he has one blue eye and one brown eye.

We talked forever when we saw each other. He told me how he got his name. He remembers when the truck driver found him and when he rode in his truck for a while. He said he was a really little baby and was quite scared. He said the truck driver named him Smokey Bear after the state policeman he knew.

He remembers the first family he lived with. They were very good to him, but for some reason they couldn't keep him.

Then he said he knew he had found his forever home when he came to live with you and Daddy. He really loved Ronnie and Kim. He said they were just kids when he lived with you all.

He said he remembered some of the not so good things he did as a little puppy. He liked to chew on things. He said he chewed on your coffee table legs and also totally rearranged your bookshelf. He said he really didn't like the taste of those books, but it was a lot of fun shredding them. However, when you and Daddy came home and saw all the mess he made, he realized you were really unhappy with him. He said you whooped him on his little bottom and told him he was doing bad things and you were not happy with him. Smokey said he was very sad that you were not happy with him. He did try to be a better boy after that book shredding adventure.

Smokey and Champ were telling all of us

about the neat kennel you and Daddy made for them. They liked being outside during the day. They always felt really safe in that special kennel. Also, they were always so happy when you all came home and brought them in the house. They loved sleeping with you and Daddy.

They loved Ronnie and Kim and loved playing with them. I told them Ronnie and Kim were all grown up when I came to live with you and Daddy. But I was always happy to have the grandchildren to love. They only came now and then for a visit, but I enjoyed the visits.

I remember you and Daddy were always so worried that Jasper or I would get out the door. You and Daddy always looked out for us. We were sure lucky boys to have you both.

Smokey and Champ said you and Daddy even had a lock on their kennel so no one could let them out to get lost. That made them feel very safe when you and Daddy were gone.

I always felt very safe when you were

gone. I just really missed you so much. I was always so happy when I heard you coming to the door.

I am so glad we found Smokey Bear. He is a really great fur brother. And he does look like a German Shepherd too.

Everyone up here told me to tell you and Daddy they send their love and kisses.

By the way, Smokey and Champ said they have another brother named Dudley. And Champ was telling me about a really sweet sister he had for many years too. He said her name was Skippy.

I will be looking them up pretty soon too. It is so much fun finding all my fur brothers and sisters. I am a very busy boy up here.

I do love it up here. It is such a great place to be. So much fun!

I hear you are going to an airport again tomorrow. I will be keeping an eye on you. Please remember, I am always with you. I have such a special place in your heart.

I love you, Sammy

A very young Smokey Bear

Our precious Dudley

Skippy was a "Daddy's Girl"
She lived out her
"Golden Years"
with Champ as her
little brother.

Hi Mommy!

I can tell you are very downhearted tonight. I saw the dream you had last night about me. You were so happy because you thought I was back with you. You thought you could make me all well.

Mommy, please remember I had a lot of things going against me down there. I was almost seventeen years old. My whole body was hurting from the arthritis. I was having trouble using my litter box. It was so hard for me to get in and out of it. I was getting confused sometimes. Dr. Jeanine even said she was starting to see the age in me. And she said she thought she felt a tumor in my bowel area. I always had a lot of IBS problems, as you know.

Those just weren't something you could have fixed. Mommy you were a wonderful Mommy and you did everything for me. You worked so hard to make me happy and comfortable. Please don't feel so bad because I am gone. I am in such a beautiful place now. I am happy. I am all healed and feel like a brand new kitty.

Remember in my last letter I told you I would be looking for Dudley and Skippy. Well, Champ saw Skippy yesterday and she is going to come to see Jasper and me real soon. She told Champ she had never had too many cats in her life before. She seems really excited to meet all of us though.

Jasper, Brittany and I hang out together all the time. We have so much fun chasing each other just like we did when we were all home with you and Daddy. But now Brittany runs really fast. She does run like a girl though.

I see you have another airport trip tomorrow. I will be watching you.

Please feel better Mommy. I love you so much and always want you to be happy.

I am sending lots of purrs and kisses to you and to Daddy.

I love you, Sammy

Hi Mommy!

I see you have had another very busy day. You sure do a lot of driving. It is so nice to watch you wherever you go. I sure am never lonesome when I can see you all through the day.

Of course, I could never be lonesome up here. There are so many wonderful friends and family to be with.

I saw Kim visiting with you and Daddy today. You all had a really nice visit. Please tell Kim I love her. I am glad you all had a good day together.

I saw her starting to cry when you read one of my letters to her. She is so very soft hearted. Please remember to tell her how happy I am up here. I know she has a few fur babies up here too. She was talking about Harley this evening. I will have to check around and see if I can find Harley for her. I am sure Harley is really happy up here too.

Today Brittany and I were telling everyone about the day Brittany came chasing me through the backyard. She was barking and running after me. I ran as fast as I could and went right through the hole in the fence. I wanted her to chase me and then I realized she couldn't get through that little hole in the fence. That was the little hole you and Daddy had made for the bunny rabbits to get through.

When she turned around and started back to you, I sneaked back through the fence and followed her very quietly all the way back to the door. She was really surprised when we ended up together again as we came back to you. We loved to chase each other. We are able to chase each other and play together every day now. I love Brittany so much.

Jasper and I are on our way to see who can catch the most butterflies this evening. We have so much fun catching them. Every one we catch gives us a kiss on our nose and then they fly away. There are so many beautiful butterflies up here. It is really good exercise for us to run after them and jump up to catch them. They love playing with all the kitties up here. Butterfly kisses are great.

Well Mommy, I will write to you again really soon. Please remember how much I love you. Brittany and Jasper said to tell you how much they love you and Daddy too.

I love you, Sammy

Our precious Sammy

Butterfly kisses anyone?

So many beautiful butterflies
to play with over the
Rainbow Bridge

Hi Mommy!

Wow! You and Daddy have been really busy. I saw you on your trip to see your friend yesterday. You and Daddy were up and out early. I am glad you were able to get away and have such a great day. It is so good that I don't have to be all alone all day when you want to go somewhere far away. I can always keep an eye on you now.

Did you like the rainbow I sent to you on your way home? I am sure you did. I was happy you liked it and knew right away it was from me. We have lots of beautiful rainbows up here. Some days when we just want to say a special "Hi" to our loved ones down there, we pick one out and send it to you. Jasper helped me pick that one out and Brittany thought it was a perfect one for you and Daddy to share while you were driving home last evening.

I did finally find Skippy. She is such a nice fur sister. She was telling me how Daddy's friend dropped her over your back yard fence. She had no idea what to expect and was pretty scared.

She said she had met Daddy when he was visiting someone in New York. They really liked each other. But she had no idea she would end up in your back yard and have you and Daddy as her forever Mommy and Daddy. She was so excited when she saw Daddy that night.

Skippy was a little worried that Champ might not like her. But she said after a few days, he decided it was fun to have a new sister. She loved living with you and Daddy and Champ. She said that Ronnie and Kim were pretty big kids when she came there. They really loved her too.

Since she was getting much older then, she was so happy to be with you all. It was a beautiful retirement home for her. She said Champ helped her feel young and she loved playing with him.

When she started feeling sick and getting so tired, she was glad you all were always there for her.

When you took her to the doctor the last time, she was so very sick. She had to leave for up here right in the middle of the night. She was sorry to leave you like that, but it just had to happen that way. She felt very loved and secure because her doctor had stayed with her all through that time. He was such a good and caring doctor. She knew how bad it made you feel, and she felt really sorry for you and Daddy and Ronnie and Kim. But she was also so happy to be up here and feel all well again. She knew you all understood and that helped her feel better too.

Skippy said she was happy to see Champ when he arrived up here. They have stayed really close and play together a lot. They both are great fur brother and sister to Jasper and me. Brittany loves playing with them too.

We are all happy here. It is so much fun finding all my fur family up here. You and Daddy have really been great fur baby parents to a lot of us. We all love you so much.

I hear you and Daddy are going to a dinner with friends this evening. I am sure you will have a good time. When you pick Aunt Judy up, please tell her I said "Hi", and send my love.

Also, please have her tell Mitzi she needs to be friends with you. She needs to trust you. You would never do anything to hurt Mitzi. She is such a pretty cat. I wonder why she is so scared of everyone. I was never scared of anyone. But I do remember how afraid Jasper was of anyone who came into the house. I always tried to reassure him that anyone you let into our house would never hurt him. He finally did get better when we had company. Mitzi sure does miss a lot of hugs and petting by being so scared. Maybe one day, just like Jasper, she will get better with visitors.

Well, I have to go. We are all meeting this evening and we are going to look up Dudley. I hear he is a very special boy. I can't wait to meet him.

I love you, Sammy

Hi Mommy!

Just wanted you to know how happy I am up here. It is just so nice. I love hearing all the birds singing. It is like a really big choir of birds. They all make different sounds and it all fits together perfectly.

Jasper has been running all around everywhere today. He loves to chase Brittany. I remember when we first got him and he would chase Brittany in circles all through the house. She was always so good at playing with him. She is a very patient girl. Today he was chasing Champ too. They have been having a really fun day.

Smokey Bear and I had a really long talk today. We think a lot alike. We both were watching you for a while. We were sorry you were feeling downhearted today. I told him how much you were missing me and how lost you were feeling.

When you left the house this morning and it was so dark and rainy, I saw you think about turning the light on for me. Just for a second you had me on your mind, because you knew how I didn't like to be in the dark. You always left the light on for me. Thank you so much for remembering the light when you would leave me.

    Thank you for still remembering me. I hope soon you can stop missing me so much. You need to just remember all the really good and fun times we had together.

    I am always with you. I am in that little part of your heart with my name on it.

SAMMY   SAMMY

    We haven't met up with Dudley yet, but when we do, I will let you know.

    Jasper just went running by here. Now he is chasing birds again. He never sits still for very long. He loves to chase the birds. They have a lot of fun with him. When he starts chasing them they fly off in different directions and he never knows which one to chase after. Then they all fly back to him and land right on his back. It is a really fun game to watch.

    Mommy, I love you and Daddy. We all

love you. Please remember, we are up here together and we are all happy. We love to be able to see what you both are doing. We just wish it was easier for you and Daddy. I can tell how lonesome you both are sometimes. Please try to feel better soon.

I love writing to you. It is so much fun meeting up with my fur brothers and sisters and being able to tell you and Daddy all about how they are doing.

We are all happy and healthy up here. It is so beautiful and peaceful here. One day, when you and Daddy come up here, we will all be together forever. That will surely be a great time for all of us.

Jasper just came back here and now he is ready to lie down for a while. He said to send his love and kisses to you.

I think I might go lie down with Jasper for a while. Maybe he could use some good purrs to help him rest.

I love you, Sammy

The Day God Took You Home

A million times
I've needed you
A million times I've cried,
If love alone
Could have saved you
you never would have died.
In life I loved you dearly,
In death I love you still.
In my heart you hold a place,
No one else can ever fill.
It broke my heart to lose you,
But you didn't go alone
Part of me went with you,
The day God took you home.

Author unknown

Hi Mommy!

Even though I have been up here for a while now, I am still keeping an eye on you and Daddy.

It is amazing that you both still stop at the door to look for me. I was such a lucky boy to have you and Daddy. You always took such good care of me. I do miss you both. However, it is really hard to miss being down there too much because life is so much fun up here. I still love you and Daddy so much.

I have been running and jumping after all the butterflies up here today. I did so many somersaults, I wasn't sure if I was up or down for a while. The butterflies really give me a lot to play with. I love all the kisses they give me on my nose.

Jasper has been running all over the place with Champ today.

Brittany and Skippy have been lying together, just watching us playing. They both just shake their heads and smile at us.

Happy and Punchy said they had spotted Dudley this morning, so we are going to look him up very soon.

They said he lives very close to a silly little girl named Missy. He seems to take care of her and hang out with her a lot up here.

I guess we will meet up with both of them soon.

Please tell Aunt Judy I hope she feels better soon. She needs to feel better so she can go to school and help the teachers when she subs for them. Tell her Jasper and Brittany and I send our love to her. Tell her to give Mitzi some hugs and kisses from all of us.

I see Daddy has been doing lots of work outside. Please let him know we all love him. He is such a good Daddy.

I will let you know when we catch up with Dudley.

I love you, Sammy

Hi Mommy!

I saw you look for me two times yesterday. Once, when you were coming in the back door with your hands full. I saw you being so careful for that moment. Then I saw the frown when you remembered you didn't have to worry about me getting out.

I also saw when you were ready to leave the house and you turned to say, "Bye Sammy. I love you. We will be right back". Yep. I saw how disappointed you were.

I have to say, you are getting better with all that stuff though. Please remember to think about all of our good times together.

I often hear you telling people some of our funny stories. That always makes me so happy.

I felt that lump in your throat this morning when the lady at your church asked you how I was doing. She was so shocked and felt really bad when you told her where I was. But no one needs to feel bad about where I am. I am in the very best place ever. I love being up here with all my fur brothers and sisters. I love the freedom. I don't feel sick anymore and I can jump and play even better than when I was a little guy. I feel really good up here.

I know those people are really feeling bad for you. Most of them know how hard it is without me by your side. Most of them have fur babies up here too.

Mommy, I am so very sorry that I had to leave you and Daddy. I know it has been really hard for you both. But I am not sorry I am here. I couldn't be any happier. I just feel good all over!

I am so happy for Jasper too. I remember how he loved to run all around the house. We could all hear him flying through the hallway. You and Daddy and Aunt Judy always called him Thunder Chicken. Then as he got older and couldn't see so good, he slowed down and had a really hard time. He couldn't run as fast as he could when he was a young boy. That really made him sad. He loved running and leaping up on his big green cat tree. Boy, he almost tipped that thing over many times when he landed on top of it. I had to run for my life a few times. I never liked being up too high. I always laid on the bottom shelf, near to the ground. But now I love watching him run so fast and he can see perfectly to land on anything he wants to land on. Also, everything up here is so much softer. No hard chairs or floors to land on. It is all soft clouds, pretty green grass and lots of trees with big beautiful leaves.

Hmmm . . . Big trees with leaves reminds me of the ones that landed in our back yard. Remember that story, Mom? That was a really exciting story that we all shared forever. Aunt Judy even wrote about that one in her book about me.

Well, we haven't met up with Dudley and Missy yet. But I think it will happen real soon. Brittany and Champ have been anxious to meet up with them too.

We all love you and Daddy.

Love, Sammy

Jasper lying on his big green cat tree.

Hi Mommy!

Wow! It has been a while since I wrote you a letter. But I have really great news! We all finally found Dudley and Missy!

Dudley is a pretty handsome guy. He told me he is a Cockapoo. He said his Mommy was a Poodle and his Daddy was a Cocker Spaniel. He is very proud of his fur parents. He told us all about how he lived with a really big girl for a few years. He said she went away to college and her parents couldn't take as good care of him as she did. They talked to a friend who knew you and Daddy. He remembered that you had said Ronnie and Kim could have a dog if it was potty trained.

Yep! Dudley fit that description. He said you came to his house to meet him and then the next day you came back and took him home to your house.

He said he was kind of scared of Kim for a while. He said her shoes made lots of noise and she moved too fast for him. She was such a little person. He was not used to little kids at all. But, as time went on he really began to love all of you. He said he was a really happy boy.

He remembers when you all had a family picture taken and you even took him with you and he was in the picture too. That made him feel really important and happy. And, Mommy, I remember that picture hanging in our bedroom. I was so happy to meet him.

One of his favorite memories with you all was the look on your faces when you would come home and find how well he had decorated the whole house with the rolls of toilet paper. He said you all would scold him, but not too hard, because you would be laughing so much. He said he did that many times. He was very disappointed when you remembered to shut the bathroom door when you all left the house.

Missy stays close to Dudley. He looks out for her up here. She doesn't remember a lot from down there. She said she saw her Mommy get hit by that really big car and remembers how sad and scared it made her feel. She and her brothers all stayed with their Mommy in that big ditch until some kids came by and found them. She was always scared and never felt happy her whole life.

She was glad those kids brought her to your house to ask if you would take her and care for her. She said she tried to be a good girl for you all, but she seemed to do a lot of things she should not do. She said she was always biting at everyone's heels and snapping at their hands when they tried to touch her. She said she was always afraid of everything.

Also, she chased the birds and killed some of them. She said that upset everyone and made her feel really bad.

Things were not working out for her down there. She remembers the doctor telling you he felt she had a really big problem and he felt it would get worse as she got bigger and older.

She was actually happy when you and Daddy made the decision to send her up here. She said the very first day up here she was all healed and very happy. And she even found her Mommy up here. That made her really happy and she felt secure and loved. No more feeling afraid all the time. This place does bring a lot of peace to everyone.

When Dudley came up here, she saw him right away and they have stayed close together all these years. They are very happy and healthy and enjoy playing together.

Dudley and Missy were so glad to meet all of us fur brothers and sisters. We had a really long visit and plan to hang around together a lot.

Oh, Mommy, there is the cutest, little white furry dog up here. He says his name is Piccolo. He told me he was your and Daddy's very first puppy. He said he was a pure bred Poodle. Wow. That sounds really important. He told me that he was a special birthday present from Daddy to you for your 21st birthday. Gee, Mommy, that was a LONG time ago.

We had a short visit the other day. He

said he had been watching me since I got up here. We have a lot in common. He was your first puppy and I was your first kitty. That makes us really special.

He said he had lots of stories to tell me and three fur brothers for me to meet. We are planning a meeting real soon.

Right now I have to go get Jasper out of a tree. He has been chasing birds all day. They have so much fun wearing him out. He fell asleep in the tree, on a big limb. So I am going to get him down and we will go take a nap with Brittany. I like naps with Brittany because they are on the ground. You know me and heights. I still prefer ground. The ground here is extra soft too.

Everyone said to tell you and Daddy how much we love you.

Love, Sammy

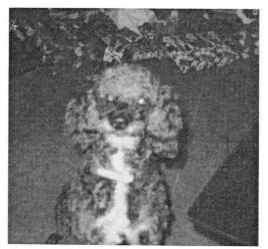

Dudley is still watching over Missy

Missy was definitely a handful
She was a very pretty girl

Hi Mommy!

Wow! I see you have really been missing me. That really loud MEEOOW, was from me. I just wanted to send my love to you. I saw you looked down beside your bed. You were so disappointed when you didn't see me. I am sorry it is still so hard for you.

When you heard the purring the other night . . . Yep, that was me. I could see you were having a hard time getting to sleep. I wanted to let you know how much I love you.

Now, that big thump against your back was The Kid. Yep. Jasper always liked to be as close to you as possible. He wanted to thump you on your back like he always used to do.

We both wanted you to feel loved and comforted so you could go to sleep. I think it did help some, because you did finally go to sleep.

I saw you were very lonely for me last evening. I know it is hard for you. But, Mommy, please try to be happy again.

I am so happy up here. Everything is just so wonderful. There is nothing bad or sad around here. Everyone and every fur baby is happy and safe. We all have so much fun playing and having great times together.

By the way, I have been thinking a lot about Aunt Judy's sister Robin. When you hear from her, please tell her I said "Hi", and I love her very much. I always loved talking to her. Robin loved me too. Tell her I will send some purrs and kitty kisses to her. Robin is a very sweet friend.

Got to run now. We are all going to meet up with Piccolo later. Maybe he will help us meet up with his other fur brothers.

Love you, Sammy

Hi Mommy!

Wow! I see you and Aunt Judy are doing another cat show. Like I told you before, I love being able to see everywhere you go now.

I was so proud of you yesterday when you were petting those cute little kittens. I know how hard that was for you. We were all watching you from up here yesterday. I also saw you when you petted and even held that really big cat. I think Bumble Bee is a strange name for a cat, but he sure is a big handsome boy. When you told Aunt Judy you thought I would have liked to have a harness like that, you were right. That would have been fun when I was younger. But I loved being just who I was with you and Daddy. You were always worried about me getting a disease or something scaring me. I am so thankful you were so careful with me. I always loved feeling so secure with you and Daddy. I loved being your special fur baby.

I hope you have fun at the cat show

today. I sure do love you.

Brittany and Jasper went with me to see Piccolo again. We all had so much fun trading stories about our lives with you and Daddy.

Piccolo said he used to love riding in the stroller with Ronnie when he was a very little baby. It is hard for me to picture Ronnie as a baby in a stroller. He was already a big grown up when I met him. Piccolo said he loved going shopping with you. He said lots of people would always stop and talk to you about what a pretty dog he was. He liked that. He is a really cute little guy. I am bigger than he is.

Well, I will let you know when I get to meet Tarzan, Jumbo and Puppy Love. Piccolo said they are all great fur brothers.

I love you, Sammy

Hi Mommy!

I saw you holding that cute little kitty at the cat show the other day. That was such a great thing that nice lady did to offer him to you for free. He sure is not a normal everyday kitty. He is a pure bred Bengal kitty. She trusted you and Daddy to take him and raise him just like you raised Jasper and me.

I know how hard it was for you and Daddy to say no to her. You both are still so lonely for me. I can feel that in you every day.

I really think that beautiful little Bengal kitten would have worn you and Daddy out. He is so full of energy. Such a nice boy, but really full of himself.

I know you and Daddy would have been perfect parents for him. But I also understand why you have decided to have no more fur babies. I really do understand, Mommy. It really bothers me when I see people trying to push another kitty on you. I know you would be great parents to another fur baby. But I know exactly how you and Daddy feel. You need to do what you think is right for you two.

I heard you talking to Aunt Judy today about me and the whole idea of another fur baby. I could see how hurt you were feeling. If I were there, I would kiss you on your nose and help you feel better. I love you so much and I do miss you and Daddy.

However, it is so much fun up here. I love being here with my fur family. We all have loved having you and Daddy as our parents. We are a very lucky bunch of fur babies.

Well, I think we will be meeting up with Piccolo soon and his special fur brothers up here. Piccolo was telling me all about Puppy Love.

Piccolo said you bought Puppy Love for two little girls as a present and they were not allowed to keep him. It was really heartbreaking for them. They were so happy when you and Daddy said you would keep him for them, and that way they could come and play with him whenever they wanted to.

Piccolo said you paid $5 for Puppy Love. I am sure he was worth much more than $5. Piccolo told me that Puppy Love was sick a lot and had to go to the doctor an awful lot of times. But he said Puppy Love really loved him and they spent a lot of time together. He was so glad you kept Puppy Love and took such good care of him.

Piccolo remembers that he was starting to feel really sick and knew it was about his time to come over the Rainbow Bridge. He tried to be really brave and not feel so sick. He wanted to stay with you and Daddy but he knew that couldn't happen.

He still remembers that day when you took him and Puppy Love to the doctor and let them both come over the Rainbow Bridge together. They both were so happy to arrive up here and feel all well again. They were so sorry to see how sad and hurt you and Daddy and Ronnie were. Piccolo said it took a really long time for you and Daddy and Ronnie to get past that sadness and hurt. He kept a pretty close eye on you all for a long time. He was so glad when you all started to feel better.

Well, Mommy, I need to go look for Jasper. He has been running around here all day. I think when I find him, we will go take a nap with Brittany.

Brittany has a really special tree that she loves to lie under. We all love taking naps there with her, all curled up together. We are all happy here. We love you and Daddy so much.

Love, Sammy

Our sweet Puppy Love

Hi Mommy

Guess what? I finally got to meet Tarzan, Jumbo and even that little guy Puppy Love. Piccolo came by the other day and brought all three of them to meet me.

Tarzan is a pretty big boy. He does look somewhat like a German Shepherd. You used to tell me I was your German Shepherd. Don't think so, Mommy. He is REALLY BIG. I think I thought a lot like a German Shepherd. But, wow, he is a LOT bigger than me.

He was telling me all about the times Jumbo jumped the fence. He said he always wanted to jump it too and go find Jumbo. He said he remembers the one time he caught his poor little front paw in the old wire fence. He said it really hurt and he did a lot of screaming until you ran out the back door and got his paw loose from the sharp fence. He was happy you got him loose. Ouch! That really did hurt him so much. He was so happy that you took such good care of it, and even took him to the doctor to make sure it didn't get infected.

Tarzan also knew Ronnie when he was a very little boy, and remembers how Ronnie couldn't say his name, so Ronnie always called him "T T". He really loved Ronnie and loved it when he called him "T T". He said you and Daddy called him "T T" also.

Wow! Jumbo still has springs in his legs! He is so pretty too. He jumps over everything up here.

He was telling me about all the times he would jump the fence and you would have to drive all over the neighborhood looking for him. He said you were pretty upset with him a few times.

He really didn't mean to get lost. He was just curious about everything going on in the neighborhood. He said he remembers the time the nice men at that garage tied him up with a long electric cord. He heard them call you on the phone. Boy, did he ever know how much trouble he was going to be in when you came to pick him up. He was really worried if he was going to get a spanking when you got him home.

Whew! He was happy when you all got home and all you did was yell at him for a while. He was really sorry that he caused all that trouble. He just couldn't control his curiosity nor the springs in his legs. He still can't!

I thought it was funny when he told me Ronnie couldn't say Jumbo, so he called him "Bo Bo". He loves that name. He said he loved you and Daddy and Ronnie so much.

He really didn't mean to piddle on that neighbor's azaleas. He thought they were just weeds. And he said he could tell that a few other dogs had felt the same way. Boy, was that man ever mad when he came to your front door. Bo Bo said he was hiding behind you while the man was yelling about him "urinating on my azaleas"! Oh, that must have been really funny to watch. Bo Bo didn't think you were very happy with him or with that really angry man. But he knew you would protect him if he hid behind you.

I also got to talk some with Puppy Love. He is such a sweet little guy. He remembers how sick he always was and how wonderful you treated him. He never liked all the doctor visits though. He said it was great being your fur baby. He said it was always nice when the two little girls came to visit him and they loved him too. He felt bad that he couldn't stay with them, but you and Daddy saved the day when you kept him so they could always have him to love. He said he always felt so loved and secure.

Puppy Love told me a funny story about that really mad neighbor man. He said one morning that man came banging on the front door again. The man was yelling about how your dogs were barking all night and had kept him awake all night. He was really mad about that.

Puppy Love said it was so funny when you told the man how strange it was that you never heard them barking. The man said he sure did hear all the barking all night long. Then he remembers you telling the man that all four of your boys were in the bed with you all night, and you were sure you would have heard them barking before he ever would.

Puppy Love was so happy telling that story. He said that man turned around and went back home. He never apologized, but he never came to your house complaining about anything again.

Mommy, Puppy Love is not sick any more, and Jumbo and Tarzan are so happy to be up here. They have all been watching you and Daddy for all these years.

Jumbo and Tarzan also remember Kim as a very little girl. They loved her and always tried to be careful and not knock her down or step on her.

Piccolo and Puppy Love said they were already up here when Kim came to live with you and Daddy and Ronnie. It was good because they were pretty small and were glad they were not around to get stepped on.

However, Jumbo does remember the time he knocked little Ronnie down the front steps. He was so scared when you all left so quick and had to take Ronnie to the hospital. He said when you came back home, Ronnie had a big bandage on his head. Jumbo felt really bad about that. He loved Ronnie so much and would never have hurt him on purpose. Those springy legs just kept getting him in trouble all the time.

Well Mommy, things up here are great. I am so happy. It is so good to meet up with all my fur brothers and sisters.

You and Daddy have had quite a big fur family. Thank you for being our Mommy and Daddy. We all really love you lots and lots.

Jasper has had a lot of fun jumping around here with Jumbo. They are good pals and have realized they both have names starting with "J", and they both love to run and jump.

They could wear anyone out. It is so good that they can run and jump and never get lost or get in trouble for having so much fun.

It has been a very busy day today. We have had so much fun. Give Daddy kisses on his nose for me.

I love you, Sammy

Jumbo – Tarzan – Piccolo
lying with Daddy

Do these pretty faces
look like they would be left
outside all night
to bark and
keep neighbors awake?

Tarzan watching out the door with his little boy, Ronnie

Hi Mommy!

It is good to see you and Daddy are starting to feel a little better. I keep watching you both every day. It is fun sometimes watching you so carefully picking up anything small you may have dropped on the floor. You are still trying to keep everything safe for me. I am safe up here, Mommy. You are such a good Mommy and Daddy. I am so glad you were my very own special parents down there. I saw Daddy pass by the bathroom and start to put the toilet lid down so I wouldn't fall in and get stuck in it. Actually, Jasper was much worse about that toilet than I was. I never had the desire to get wet in any fashion. Jasper was just much too curious about everything. He still is. He is always climbing trees and jumping all through the pretty bushes up here. I am so happy that he has a lot of soft clouds to catch him when he jumps off the tree limbs. I swear he must think he can fly. Well, maybe he could fly up here. That sort of stuff is mostly left up to the angels that are up here. There are really pretty angels up here. Most of us fur babies stay pretty close to the soft ground. It is soft and green and so beautiful.

Well, Mommy, we are all going to have a family reunion up here pretty soon. We have all met and had lots of talks about our lives down there with you and Daddy. So now, we are going to get everyone up here together all at one time for a really big celebration.

It is going to be a lot of fun. I will be sure and write you a long letter and tell you how much fun we will be having.

I see it is starting to be Fall time down there. That brings back a lot of memories for me. That is the time I came looking for a new home.

My other home had put me outside because they had a new human baby and they were afraid I would hurt him. That was such a silly thought. I would have loved him and would have taken very good care of him.

Oh well, I am so happy that I found Brittany watching me in the window. She was so sweet to me and really wanted me to come in and live with her. She knew it would all work out for the best for all of us. It did!

I always loved Fall because that was when I came to live with you and Daddy and Brittany. And Aunt Judy kept opening the bathroom window and letting me in the house. She was so funny. I sure do love Aunt Judy. She sure does love her fur baby Mitzi. Mitzi is one very pretty girl. Aunt Judy spoils her just like you and Daddy always spoiled all of us fur babies.

I will be watching you decorate the house. I guess you can do a good job without my help this year. I always loved dragging those silk leaves all over the living room. Some of them were good for chewing on too. I will miss helping you this year, but I will be watching you very closely.

I love you, Sammy

Jasper

Our precious boys
Just chillin'

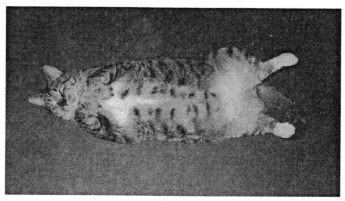

Sammy

Hi Daddy!

I bet you are surprised to hear from me! I just wanted to let you know how much I love you.

I see Mommy and Aunt Judy are at a cat show. They are having a good day with their friends.

I have been watching you today. Daddy, you are always so busy. I often wondered what you were doing when you kept going in and out the door so many times during the day. Now I can watch you.

I see you are moving all that furniture out of the garage. I wonder why you are taking it away to your other garage so far away. I guess you have a good reason. It is so much easier for you to go in and out the door now.

I can tell you still miss me a lot. But you and Mommy are getting better. I am glad you are not so sad now.

Please try not to work too hard. Mommy always wants you to rest and take care of yourself. I do too. That is why I always wanted you to lie down with me on the bed. It gave us a chance to cuddle and it made you rest for a little while.

Jasper and Brittany are here with me today. They both said to send their love. They want to let you know what a good Daddy you always were. They still love you very much.

Brittany still remembers all those times in the winter when it snowed, you would use your snow blower and make nice paths for her to use when she had to go out to do her business. She didn't like getting so much snow caught in her paws. You were so good at cleaning her off when she came back in from being in the snow. That always made her so happy.

We all have been talking about how hard you always work. You always told us it was so you and Mommy could buy food for us. But now you don't have to feed us. We are all well fed up here. But you are still working extra hard.

I love you Daddy. I miss your hugs and belly rubs. You were so good at that. Thank you for all your love through all those years. I am so glad I won you over. I was one special kitty in your life. Jasper was such a special silly baby too. We really did make you a believer in kitty love.

Brittany was talking about all the baths and great haircuts you gave her over her whole life. She always was so happy when you got finished and she looked so pretty and smelled so good.. Oh, Daddy, she is still so beautiful and she always smells just perfect. We are so glad to be back together again.

Brittany and Jasper send their love and kisses to you. Please don't work too hard. We hope you like our letter to you. We love you.

Love, Sammy

A very young Brittany
with her girl, Kim

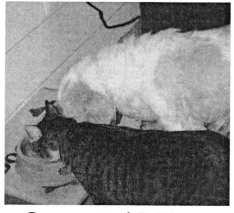

Sammy and Brittany
sharing dinner

Hi Mommy!

I see you have the house all decorated for Fall now. It looks really nice. You did a good job without my help this year.

I remember that very first night you and Aunt Judy brought me in the house because you were afraid the Trick or Treaters would hurt me, or I would get lost.

I was so happy to be in the nice warm house with Brittany. I had always wanted to be with her inside the house. I was on my way to winning everyone over and I knew it.

Thank you for caring so much about me and my safety. I always knew every year when Halloween came around it was my anniversary of being your special kitty. Having all those kids come to the door was exciting because I knew the other holidays were coming really soon too.

I know Thanksgiving was your favorite holiday. You always made the house smell so good. Of course, Jasper was always trying to help you cook the turkey. He really loved the smells in the kitchen, especially the turkey.

By the way, please tell Kim that I met Harley the other day. She is a really big girl. She is so pretty too. We were talking about how nice it is to be up here. She said she was really sick for some time before she made her trip up here. She sure isn't sick any more. She is all well and happy. Harley said to let Kim know she misses everyone, but there is just so much to do up here and everything is fun and she is so happy.

Harley can really run fast. She is so big, it is hard for her to get stopped sometimes. Her hair is beautiful and so soft. She is a pretty red color. Please tell Kim that Harley sends her love to her and Ryan and Tyler. Harley is a very happy and loving girl.

Well, Mom, we are thinking we will have our family reunion up here on Thanksgiving this year. We are all planning on getting together then because we are all so thankful to be up here. We are all well and happy and so glad you and Daddy were our parents. We all had really good lives with you and Daddy. So we are going to celebrate in honor of you and Daddy on Thanksgiving since that is your favorite holiday.

Yep, the house is looking really nice for Fall. You did a great job. I will be staying close with my purrs.

I love you, Sammy

P.S. Did you know that every day is Thanksgiving Day up here. Yep. We are thankful for everything every day. It is so wonderful.

Sweet, precious Harley

Hi Daddy!

It's me again! I found someone very special up here today. Actually, I found two special fur babies.

This really handsome black and white dog heard us talking about having a Maxson family reunion. He said he remembered that name from a very long time ago. He said he was your fur baby when you were just a little kid. Wow! That must have been a VERY LONG time ago!

His name is Old Joe. He remembers growing up for several years with you and some of your brothers and sisters. He said you all lived on a farm and he had lots of fun playing with all of you. He loved you the best. He said you were so loving to him. He has been up here for a really long time.

He loves it here and was very glad to hear about all the fur babies you have had over your life.

He always thought cats were just good for chasing all over the farm. Then when he came up here, he found out how nice cats are. He likes me. We have become good friends.

I also met the cutest little black puppy. He said he remembered living with you for a little while when you were a little kid too. He said he wasn't with you for a very long time though. His name is Blackie.

He is sure you would remember him. He said that everyone was moving from the farm and when he got in the car someone stopped along the road and put him out of the car right along the busy road.

He was so little and really scared as the car drove away. He was worried that you would miss him and wonder where he was, but there was no way to find you again. He started running through a really big field. His little heart was pounding with fear. After a while, he just laid down in the field to rest. He had no idea what to do or where to go.

While he was lying there all quiet, he could hear voices pretty near to him. When he looked up over the weeds, he saw two kids playing on a tractor that was sitting in the field. At first he was really scared and just laid there and watched them. They were about the same size you were at the time, so he figured maybe they would like him too.

When he started walking toward them, they saw him and were so excited. They ran to him and picked him up. He was so relieved and happy to see they liked him.

They took him to their house and from then on, he was their puppy. He always wondered what happened and why he never made it on that move to be with you again. But he was content to be loved by his new family. He lived with them for many years. When he finally came up here, he began to understand why things happened the way they did. He was just so thankful that those kids loved him and he had a good home.

What he thought was so neat is the new kids named him Blackie also. That made him really happy. He said to tell you that he had a really great life and he never has forgotten you. I told him you were the best Daddy in the whole world. He loves being up here and is planning on meeting up with all the rest of your fur babies.

Yep, Old Joe and Blackie are both doing just fine up here, and both send their love to you.

You are one very special Daddy.

I love you, Sammy

Old Joe with his little boy,
(Best Daddy in the whole world)

Hi Mommy!

I see it is Halloween tonight. That always brings good memories for me. I can watch you when you give the candy out to the Trick or Treaters. I don't have to stay in the bedroom. I like being able to see everyone.

That first Halloween night way back, when you and Aunt Judy brought me in the house was one of my most favorite memories. I loved being in the house with Brittany and you and Aunt Judy. I felt so loved and it made me feel really secure too.

We don't have Halloween up here. But we all have fun watching it all from up here. So many little kids that are all dressed up to go Trick or Treating. Most of us have had little kids in our lives and really love watching them.

Brittany was telling all of us about some of the Halloweens you all had when you went camping. She said you put real baby clothes on her and she was even in a playpen. She really loved that. She was always a really good sport.

Well, Mom, I need to go. I am making plans for our family reunion. It is going to be so much fun.

By the way, the house really does look nice. I see you have the outside decorated too. It does make it look like Fall all over.

Jasper and Brittany send kisses to you and to Daddy.

I love you, Sammy

Very young Sammy and Jasper

Hi Mommy!

Gee! It sure has been busy up here. Sorry I haven't written to you in a while.

We are working on our family reunion. Happy and Punchy have been flying all around making sure all of the family knows where to get together.

Thanksgiving is only a couple of weeks away. We are planning on having lots of good food. We are going to play some really neat games too.

The butterflies and birds have said they will help us with some chasing games. That will be a lot of fun. The prizes will be butterfly kisses.

Missy was glad to know she can chase butterflies and birds up here and not hurt them. She always had a problem with that down there.

Oh, Mommy, I am so excited. Our reunion will be so much fun. Jasper and Jumbo are trying to figure out some jumping games. Of course, that is their specialty.

Brittany and Skippy are planning the

menu. I am sure it will all be great food.

Smokey Bear said he hoped we would have stuffed green peppers. He really loved your stuffed green peppers. He told us the story about you dropping a plate full of stuffed green peppers. Smokey said you caught the plate, but one stuffed green pepper landed on the floor right in front of him. He didn't want your carpet to get stained, so he woofed it down in an instant. He said you were really shocked. Smokey has always wanted stuffed green peppers ever since.

He told us all about the chocolate brownies he ate while you all were at church. That was not a very funny story. He said he got very sick. He did learn a lesson about chocolate and dogs. Yuck. I am glad I wasn't around for that mess. I am sure there will be no chocolate at our reunion. I wouldn't want any problems up here. Fur babies should never have chocolate, whether down there or up here.

Jasper just flew by here with Jumbo right on his heels. The problem there is when

Jasper stops really quick, Jumbo goes head over heels trying to stop. They are so funny to watch.

Well, Mom, I need to go. Brittany and Skippy need my help to figure out the food for our reunion. We can all eat the same food up here. It isn't for cats or for dogs, it is good food for everyone.

Give Daddy some kisses on his nose. We all love you and Daddy so much.

Love, Sammy

Sammy and Jasper patiently waiting outside my office door.

Precious Jasper

Sammy and Jasper were always close together.

Hi Mommy!

I am so excited! Our reunion is only two days away! We are all so excited to be together for such a great celebration.

I have been watching down there too. I saw Aunt Judy in your office today. It was so funny to watch her look for me when she went out of your office door. I usually was lying outside your door, or on the bed. She actually caught herself checking for me. It has been a long time since I came up here, but I seem to still be on everyone's mind. That makes me feel so special.

I see you are almost ready for your Thanksgiving Day down there. At least you can fix your turkey without all the EXTRA help you got from Jasper and me. While you are fixing your dinner down there, we will be celebrating our fur family up here.

Mommy, I am so glad your favorite holiday is Thanksgiving. That is such a special day.

As you probably remember, my favorite holiday was and is Christmas. It was and is

Jasper's favorite holiday too. We both always loved Christmas the best. We had so much fun HELPING you decorate the house.

I always loved the red bells you put on the bottom of the tree for me to play with. They made such a great noise, and they were RED, my favorite color.

I had a hard time after Jasper left us. Christmas just was not as much fun. I missed him SO MUCH. I know you and Daddy tried so hard to help me and make me happy. I was always so thankful for your love and understanding. I knew you and Daddy missed him too.

It is so wonderful to be back together with Jasper and Brittany. I am one very happy boy.

We are all sorry that you and Daddy are all alone now, but we aren't too far away. If you listen closely you can still hear our purrs. We all love you both so much.

Well, I need to go. There is so much going on up here today. Happy and Punchy have been hanging ribbons all over the place. We are all planning on meeting at

Brittany's favorite tree. It is really pretty there and we can hang our ribbons all over the tree and all the bushes around it.

Of course all the ribbons are going to be RED, my favorite color.

I am so glad to see you and Daddy are beginning to feel better. That makes me very happy.

We all love you and Daddy very much.

Love, Sammy

Sammy and Jasper
just being together

Definite Soul Mates

Hi Mommy!

Just a quick note from up here. I sure can smell that wonderful Thanksgiving dinner you are cooking. Jasper said he could smell turkey all over the place up here. We love watching you enjoy your special holiday.

Our family reunion will be starting in just a little while. We have everything all ready to start. We have lots of food ready. Brittany and Skippy have done a great job with the food. I don't want to tell Jasper, but we are having turkey up here today. Shhh . . . Jasper will be so surprised.

Oh, Mommy, I am so happy! This has been so exciting to put our reunion all together. We invited all our fur brothers and sisters to come. I think a few others will be coming too. We invited Harley to join us. She said she would be happy to come to our reunion.

Of course, we invited Old Joe and Blackie. I am sure they will be here too. I personally invited Kitty to stop by too. He said he would probably come. I hope he does stop by, at least for a while. Remember, Kitty is that pretty orange cat that the nice man wrote about in his book. I am so glad we made friends. Like I said before, orange is good.

    I am getting so excited and I need to go help Brittany and Skippy.

    Geesh! Jasper and Jumbo just ran past here. They are practicing for the games we are going to play later today, as if they need any practice running.

    Please enjoy your Thanksgiving dinner and tell everyone we all send our love and kisses to them.

    I will let you know how everything turns out. I am sure it will all be perfect. Everything up here is perfect every day.

I love you, Sammy

Hi Mommy!

The reunion was totally awesome! We all had so much fun. Everyone played games and we all got to know each other better than ever.

We played, "catch a butterfly", and we all played "chase a bird". That was so neat. Those birds had so much fun watching all of us falling all over each other trying to catch them. Happy and Punchy made great friends with other birds up here too. We all laughed and laughed at how at how funny we all looked sprawled out all over the grass up here.

Jasper and Jumbo both won the jumping game. They each jumped over the special bushes we had marked off with red ribbons. They were really high bushes. It was more fun to watch than when Jasper tried to land on his big green cat tree at home. I didn't have to run for my life.

Jasper was so happy when he found out we were having turkey at our dinner today. He kissed Brittany and Skippy all over their noses. He will smell like turkey for a while. Of course, he ate more turkey than anyone else. We had lots of other food too. I am so glad he can eat so much and not have to worry about his tummy hurting anymore.

Mommy, it was so perfect. I knew it would be. We still have red ribbons all over the place up here. I am so happy.

Thank you and Daddy for having such a great fur family. We all love you and Daddy so much. You and Daddy helped all of us accept and love each other. Being up here together is such a blessing. We are never alone. It is wonderful.

I saw you all had a great day too. I am so happy that you and Daddy are starting to feel better. It does take time. I know you will never forget me or any of us up here. We are all such a big part of your hearts.

Thank you for loving us so much.

I love you, Sammy

Hi Mommy!

Wow! It has been a long time since I have written to you. I have been really busy and I noticed you and Daddy have been really busy too.

I can see you are starting to put your Fall decorations away. I know you will be putting your Christmas tree up and all your Christmas decorations too. I saw you looking through your closet for your decorations. You put that big roll of RED ribbon out. That made me smile. I guess I will ALWAYS love RED ribbon.

Please be sure to put those red bells on the tree. I still would love to see them on the tree.

I know it will be hard for you this Christmas, but remember that I am watching you all the time. I love you and Daddy.

Well, I will be going for now. I am planning to take a nap with Brittany. Jasper is already lying with her. They were both curled up under her special tree. It looks inviting, so I will go join them.

I love you, Sammy

Sammy and Jasper both
Loved to watch over the Nativity

Hi Mommy!

I see that you have finally finished decorating your Christmas tree and you have the house looking really nice.

I watched you decorate the tree with those RED BELLS. I also saw your tears when you put the ornaments on the tree with Jasper and my pictures on them. I am sorry you felt so bad. You still put the ornament for Brittany on too. We all love you, Mommy. We will be watching you so close. When you are still , and watching the lights on the tree, you will probably hear us purring for you.

I remember that plastic Nativity scene you always put in the living room. Jasper loved to sit in it and I always loved to watch the people and the animals too.

Now I know who those people are. Now I know what that scene means. I knew there was something special about that part of Christmas. It is all clear to me now. It makes me happy to know what the real meaning of Christmas is.

On Christmas Day up here, we are having a really big Birthday Party. Everyone is invited. It will be a great celebration. We have all been told the special story, and we are looking forward to the celebration.

Well, Mom, please tell Daddy how much we love him. We all send kisses to you and to Daddy.

I guess you will be celebrating Christmas down there the same time we will be celebrating up here. We just have an awesome front row seat.

I will write more to you before Christmas.

I love you, Sammy

One of Sammy and Jasper's first Christmases together

Sammy loved the Christmas tree

Sammy supervising the decorating of the front porch

Jasper's special Frank E. Post

Hi Mommy & Daddy!

Well, it is Christmas Eve. We are all getting ready for the big Birthday Party up here tomorrow. Christmas Day will be a big celebration day. Everyone is so happy. We all feel so blessed to be here, and be part of such a wonderful celebration.

I have been watching you both. I can see how much you are missing me. I hope you feel better soon. I am really proud of how well you have done so far. Just remember, I am in the best place in the whole world. I love being here with all my fur brothers and sisters. We all love each other and we all love you both.

Christmas is such a special time, and we have all talked about our Christmases with you and our family down there. We all have great memories of our Christmases. You both always made it a wonderful time for us.

Jasper told me he saw you put batteries in Frank E. Post this year. Jasper loves Frank E. Post, and he has loved watching him sing this year.

Jasper and I both love that Nativity Scene. It looks so nice in the living room.

Life is so good up here. We are so happy to be all together. We love you both and we all want to wish you a very

MERRY CHRISTMAS !!

We love you,
Sammy
Jasper
Brittany
Skippy
Champ
Smokey Bear
Missy
Dudley
Puppy Love
Tarzan
Jumbo
Piccolo
Old Joe
Blackie
Harley
Happy & Punchy

Sammy's Fur Family

Young Sammy

Mature Sammy

A NOTE ABOUT SAMMY

Sammy was and is a very famous cat. Sammy has several books written about him and they have been sold all over the United States and in several other countries.

Sammy was never just a regular cat. He showed his extreme intelligence many times over his life. We began to call him our College Professor. He definitely deserved that title.

Books written about Sammy
by his Aunt,
Judy S. Walter

Sammy, the Talking Cat

Sammy Goes On Tour

The Grey and White Stranger
(features Sammy also)

Sammy's Mommy and Daddy

Penny Maxson and husband, Ron